Let's Make a Deal

**ROADMAPS
TO SUCCESS**

The Practicing Administrator's Leadership Series
Jerry J. Herman and Janice L. Herman, Editors

Other Titles in This Series Include:

(see back cover for additional titles)

Let's Make a Deal

Collaborating on a Full-Service School With Your Community

Susan Hoover
Charles M. Achilles

CORWIN PRESS, INC.
A Sage Publications Company
Thousand Oaks, California

For information address:

Corwin Press, Inc.
A Sage Publications Company
2455 Teller Road
Thousand Oaks, California 91320
email: order@corwin.sagepub.com

SAGE Publications Ltd.
6 Bonhill Street
London EC2A 4PU
United Kingdom

SAGE Publications India Pvt. Ltd.
M-32 Market
Greater Kailash I
New Delhi 110 048 India

Printed in the United States of America

Library of Congress Cataloging-in-Publication Data

Hoover, Susan.
    Let's make a deal : collaborating on a full-service school with
your community / Susan Hoover, Charles M. Achilles.
        p.   cm. — (Roadmaps to success)
    Includes bibliographical references (pp. 49-54).
    ISBN 0-8039-6346-7 (pbk. : alk. paper)
    1. Community and school—United States—Handbooks, manuals, etc.
    2. School social work—United States—Handbooks, manuals, etc.
    3. School improvement programs—United States—Handbooks, manuals,
etc.   I. Achilles, Charles M.   II. Title.   III. Series.
    LC221.H66   1996
    370.19'31'0973—dc20   95-47185

This book is printed on acid-free paper.

96 97 98 99 00 10 9 8 7 6 5 4 3 2 1

Corwin Press Production Editor: S. Marlene Head

Contents

Foreword

Susan Hoover and Chuck Achilles write about a "full-service school." By this, they mean a school and community collaborative effort that is focused on the improvement of the benefits that are provided to the youngsters of a school district. They outline, as an example, the cooperative efforts of the Bryson Middle School and the Piedmont Center for Mental Health in Greenville County, South Carolina; together, these two institutions developed a school-based mental health delivery model titled Families and Neighborhood Schools (FANS).

Chapter 1 makes the case for schools and communities working together for students. Chapter 2 provides data related to the FANS case study. Chapter 3 highlights 10 steps to achieving a collaborative effort. Chapter 4 provides a list of common denominators among various innovative approaches to school and community collaboration taken from exemplary programs in place in the United States. Chapter 5 presents a glimpse into the reasons why collaboration between schools and communities is necessary to improve the future for students.

The authors clearly believe schools do not exist in an environmental vacuum. This book is a helpful resource for everyone who believes that it is necessary to involve the school *and* the community in raising and educating the whole child.

JERRY J. HERMAN
JANICE L. HERMAN
Series Co-Editors

Acknowledgments

The authors gratefully acknowledge all who assisted in this story of collaboration, especially the educators who promote the welfare of youth. To other professionals engaging in collaborative school ventures, we applaud both your tenacity and your recognition that education can't be just "business as usual."

Special thanks go to Dr. Joseph Bevilacqua, Joe James, and Dr. Gary Melton for their undaunting spirits as caregivers. Linda Smith and Vicki Fanning unselfishly gave FANS its glue to unite the worlds of caring and giving.

We appreciate the educators of Nova Southeastern University and The Greenville County School District for promoting action research and for supporting the FANS initiative. Thank you, Dr. David Vickery and Marshall Nichols, for your special encouragement of Susan Hoover.

To our families, bless your loving patience. Many heartfelt thanks go to Helen Pratt, Joanna Warder, and Ruth George for enduring friendship, supportive counsel, and lots of hard work. Finally, to students everywhere, we thank you and hope that your lives are filled with teaching, learning, and sharing.

SUSAN HOOVER
CHARLES M. ACHILLES

About the Authors

Susan Hoover has taught high school English and yearbook production, served as a K-12 gifted and talented education coordinator, and directed an alternative program for at-risk students. Since 1985, she has been a middle and high school principal in Greenville, South Carolina, where she also serves on the Board of Directors of the Upstate Mediation Network, Piedmont Residential Homes Placement, and South Carolina Children's Advisory Committee. As principal, she initiated Families and Neighborhood Schools (FANS) at Bryson Middle School and the SMART Team (Students Making Alternative Resolutions Together) school-community program at Woodmont High School, one of South Carolina's first sanctioned peer mediation conflict resolution plans. She has helped promote replication of FANS in schools throughout South Carolina and presented the FANS and SMART stories to groups such as the American Association of School Administrators (AASA), the American Educational Research Association (AERA), MetLife, and the University Council for Educational Administration (UCEA).

Hoover received her B.S. in English from Appalachian State University in Boone, North Carolina, her M.A. from Furman University in Greenville, South Carolina, and her doctorate in educational leadership from Nova Southeastern University in Fort Lauderdale, Florida.

Charles M. Achilles is a generalist who has researched school issues, including desegregation, effective schools, public confidence, educational cooperatives, preparation of administrators, and class-size effects on pupil achievement and development in primary grades. He is coauthor of three other books with Corwin Press: *Finding Funding; Grantwriting, Fundraising, and Partnerships;* and *Handbook on Gangs in Schools.*

Currently Professor of Educational Leadership at Eastern Michigan University, he was Professor and Department Chair at the University of North Carolina at Greensboro. He worked more than 20 years in educational administration and at the Bureau of Educational Research and Services at the University of Tennessee, Knoxville. He served at the (former) U.S. Office of Education and as a researcher at the University of California, Berkeley, after teaching in public and private schools. As a lecturer for Nova Southeastern University, he meets educators on the front lines from whom he learned about programs described in this volume.

Achilles holds an A.B. in classics, an M.A. in education and Latin, and an Ed.S. and Ed.D. in educational administration, all from the University of Rochester, New York.

Introduction

Shared Problems and Shared Solutions

The topics addressed in this book—ideas relating to a "full-service" school to benefit young people through community and school cooperation—are not new. What is new is the current view of (a) *why* the idea of a full-service school is important now, (b) *what* we now know about what may and may not work, and (c) *how* to make such cooperation effective.

Large-scale and nationally recognized collaborative efforts, such as the Comer School Improvement Process and the Coalition of Essential Schools, are available as models. Some people, however, may desire a more "down home" and personal sense of the current push for the full-service school idea; they may wish to start local initiatives. This primer for collaboration is a roadmap for success with a local approach.

Personnel at Bryson Middle School and the Piedmont Center for Mental Health in Greenville County, South Carolina collaborated to organize and evaluate the state's first school-based mental health delivery model titled Families and Neighborhood Schools (FANS). The FANS initiative serves as a prototype for ideas provided in this book.

National demographics portray a bleak picture of the condition of school-age and younger youth. Hodgkinson (1991) refers to increasing poverty as "education's leaking roof" (p. 9). The teacher is faced with an increasingly difficult task in educating today's youth yet may not even know what is really going on in a child's life: visits to social services or health or mental health departments; stipulations from a judge or department of juvenile justice (e.g., probation or parole); or home trauma (divorce, abuse). When this child is in a classroom, the general ("statistical") problem becomes individual and personal. Worse, services that a child needs to be ready for education may not be connected to the education process; educators may not know the child's involvement with other agencies. Services to children are often isolated from each other.

School buildings are located conveniently throughout most communities. They may have extra space, or space underused at certain times; often, they are located on public bus routes. They are public places. Logically, school facilities can be used to house other human services that complement and support education. But there is more: The education and other services can be coordinated to achieve goals of each system, and the school can serve as the hub for the delivery of various services.

The American Association of School Administrators (AASA) supports the collaborating of educators and others to improve education. The 1995 AASA *Platform and Resolutions* addresses collaboration directly in the category "Relationships With Other Organizations and Agencies": "AASA urges and supports collaborative, community-wide programs and the delivery of full service programs to address the needs of children" (AASA, 1995, p. 16).

Why?

Assembly Lines:
Inefficient, Ineffective, Inhuman

Today's Dinosaurs

Toffler and Toffler (1995) speak of education and health in the same breath when discussing the moribund second-wave institutions of American society. They see education and health as "massifying" the services they provide in a smokestack, assembly-line procedure. However, they believe that in the third wave, there will be stronger roles for families and that useful, multiorganizational events will lead toward structures that some people might initially confuse for large-scale, second-wave institutions. But these new conglomerates really can "demassify" procedures. In their futuristic view of the coming millennium, the Tofflers argue persuasively that old bureaucratic procedures, with separate and huge bureaucracies for each procedure, are today's dinosaurs. Amen!

Gardner (1995) argues that "a vital community reconciles group purposes for individual diversity" and points out that "the goal is to achieve wholeness incorporating diversity" (p. 25). In developing wholeness by incorporating diversity, "we must regenerate the sense of community from the ground up" (p. 25). Collaboration, the operationalizing of cooperation to expand the successful achievement of the goals of all involved parties, is the embodiment of a sense of community.

It is a challenge to combine the Tofflers' ideas of smallness, of demassifying society, and other third-wave issues in constructing Gardner's sense of community. One goal is to have coordinated services available to people who need them *without* establishing new dinosaurs; to ensure accountability without hierarchies that fall by their own weight.

In the old model, to get services from the Health Department, a person had to go to the Health Department and work with that bureaucracy. Likewise, for education, the person had to go to school and work with that bureaucracy. A person should be able to visit one convenient place to receive services of multiple agencies. Enter here the single-site, full- service school built on the common-sense idea that some services support each other and are logically provided together. Reciprocity is important; a collaborative activity benefits each partner in some logical and important way.

In moving to collaborate, some people will try to reestablish the second-wave structures and bureaucracies that comforted them in the past. The real test is KISS—"Keep It Simple Somehow." Apocryphal or not, stories of fund-raising charities that spend most of the funds they raise on fund-raising and administrative costs are instructive. This dilemma can happen if those in charge spend so much time establishing structures and calling meetings that the collaborative's work does not get done.

Yet there is a need for some structure and for records of what occurs. Seeking the proper balance is much like building an airplane while flying it, except that in building collaboratives, this "go and do" way is probably correct. Major impediments to collaborative activity are the talking, the philosophizing, and the turf tussles. Get something started; work on it to learn its complexities. This does not deny the need to establish goals and common grounds for the collaboration. Barnett (1995) expressed the necessity of such things as strategic planning or "visioning" to set directions for collaborative activity. Barnett's guidelines and information are useful. Once contacts have been made and some work has begun cautiously, there will be time to sharpen and refine what is going on. People will then see benefits to meetings. Busy people resent being overinvolved (High, Achilles, & High, 1984).

Walking the Talk

Although there is considerable talk about collaborative activity, there is little research on collaboration or its benefits to students. Action research done at the site can help with evaluations of program successes. Knapp (1995) has suggested several ways of strengthening studies of collaborative services. The studies should be "strongly conceptualized, descriptive, comparative, constructively skeptical . . . and (when appropriate) collaborative" (p. 5). At the start of one collaborative discussed here, Families and Neighborhood Schools (FANS), the evaluation/research activity was designed to find out if, in fact, the services provided the desired results for participants. Although not a highly sophisticated study, research showed that changes were in the desired direction, clients were satisfied, all parties benefited from the collaborative, and costs were reasonable and reduced (Hoover, 1992).

A Working Definition

The concept behind collaboration derives from its Latin roots. To collaborate is to work together. The National School Boards Association (1993) said it well: "Collaboration involves cooperative efforts by parties with similar or overlapping objectives to reach goals that cannot be achieved by either party acting alone" (p. 3). Collaboration is more than letting some agency use a facility; it requires collegial action to achieve common purposes and goals.

Change—A Permanent Condition

"What goes around, comes around," and "the more things change, the more they stay the same." Common expressions sometimes explain similarities that seem cyclical. But on careful examination, they may hide important differences, such as context—including advances in science and technology—and demographic changes. Cooperation in education is not new. The focus and urgency may be different today than in the past. Much in the "new" movement toward today's full-service school resembles the community school and "lighted schoolhouse" (e.g., see Harris & Harris, 1980).

Beyond the community education/community school movement, there are many other cooperative endeavors. Hughes, Achilles, Spence, and Leonard (1971) analyzed cooperative structures and activities in education, including education cooperatives, special-purpose groupings (such as special educational or vocational services), and long-standing business-education cooperation. Seeley (1981) spoke to the need for and successes of cooperation and partnerships in education. Arthur and Bauman (1994) commented on school-business-community partnerships, school-university partnerships, school-parent-community partnerships, and school/public agency partnerships. Many education improvement initiatives (e.g. Comer Model, Safe Haven, Head Start) incorporate mental health services, social services, or both as part of the intervention.

Searching for the "Lost Generation"

Many youth in school and those about to enter the education system represent America's "lost youth generation"—a generation with declining home and family stability, religious training, and understanding of the values of the past; a generation with increasing poverty, violence, disregard for human life, attraction to technology and media, and so on. The *why, where,* and *when* elements of the problem are well defined. The *what* and *how* questions remain to be clarified and answered. Schools will never be like Lake Wobegone, where all the children are above average, but we ought to strive for this goal. *Educators cannot do this job alone!*

In presenting this "search party" material, we relied on some field studies and action research to show the efficacy of collaboration. We synthesized ideas from the expanding knowledge base on collaboration. We interviewed people who are doing things that seem important. Part of the presentation is a first-person narrative showing the tensions and joys of collaboration.

What?

The Same But Different

Collaboration as Part of Restructuring

"Restructuring" is currently tossed around as a generic cure for public schools. Educators are told to change course offerings, to be "global"; to change time use with block schedules, extended day, and extended year; and to adopt or adapt business strategies presumably designed to make education more efficient. Although the options are varied, they are pointless without one element needed to make schools stronger—inviting the community to help educators identify and address social issues that are tearing at community students, luring them from traditional educational and community values, and producing violent, turbulent times for American schools. Mitchell and Beach (1993) advocate "redefining the school service mix" (p. 255) to include adjusting the school mission and to expand school-based service delivery to students and others. *Quit tinkering; just do it!*

To build strategies to increase student involvement and participation in school and to alleviate the social stresses affecting student achievement, educators are coming to envision the schoolhouse as a human service delivery center for coordinated applications of, for example, social, health, employment, and recreation services at a single site. Questions remain: "Can school and community collaboration produce results that positively affect students' lives?" and "Do such programs detract from or support the academic mission of the school?" *Education today can't be "the same-old same-old."*

The Collaborators

One System's Reaction

Greenville County, South Carolina (SC) has demographic problems similar to the national picture. Rather than continuing business as usual, some educators and others there took direct action to make a difference in schools, students' lives, and community involvement. These efforts resulted in innovative school programs that promote a renewed sense of community and that effectively serve the emotional, social, and academic needs of middle and high school students.

People at Bryson Middle School (student population = 1,200) and Woodmont High School (student population = 900) have incorporated school and community agendas to address the human service needs affecting students' academic achievement. To improve student welfare, programs have united a community resource group that includes members of the Greenville County School District; Piedmont Mental Health Center; State Departments of Mental Health, Human Health and Services, Social Services, Education, and Juvenile Justice; MetLife Education Foundation; Manpower Development Corporation; SC Public Radio Network; Upstate Mediation Network; SC Council for Mediation and Alternative Dispute Resolution; National Association for Mediation in Education; South Carolina Bar Association; Greenville County Sheriff's Department; Greenville County Solicitor's Office; local churches and businesses; and dozens of students and parents.

FANS was a collaborative effort to provide holistic community agency service to students and families as an integrated part of a school-based mental health program. Before developing FANS, collaborators took a long, hard look at *who* the school's clients were in Greenville County, *how* they live, and *what* forces may have impeded their educational progress. They believed that for people to understand the importance of new arrangements to help with schooling, people must understand the bigger picture in Greenville, one that resembles many hometowns. Facts about Greenville County and South Carolina are derived from *A Kids Count Report on the Status of Children in South Carolina, 1993* (South Carolina Department of Education, 1993), but similar statistics are available to help educators elsewhere understand local problems. The pertinent facts for Greenville are categorized and supported with brief examples. A similar environmental scan at each site where people are contemplating collaborative efforts is a good way to identify needs and set directions.

Descriptions of Value

- According to the 1990 census, 78% of Greenville's mothers with children ages 6-17 were in the labor force, and most fathers worked.

Abuse and Neglect in Greenville County

- From 1990 to 1992, approximately 1,600 children were involved in reported cases of abuse and neglect.

Demise of the Traditional Family

- In 1990, 4% of children did not live with either natural parent.
- Births to single mothers were up from 8% in 1960 to 24% in 1991; percentages were higher for non-Anglo children.

Poverty and Income in Greenville County

- In 1989, more than 14% of children lived below the poverty line.

Youth and Crime Relationships

- During 1991, more than 600 youths aged 15 to 17 (about 15%) were referred to family court. The National Youth

Survey indicated that across the United States, the number of youths engaging in some crime is two or three times the number apprehended.

School Readiness, Failure Rates, and Special Education Rates

- In 1991, 27% of children were not ready for first grade.
- In 1992, 14% of first-grade children were failing.
- Approximately 11% of all students in Grades 1 to 12 during 1991 were being served in special education classes.

The Summary Status of Greenville County Typically Reflects a Dramatically Changing American Society, One No Longer Only "Traditional"

- 22% of children lived in single-parent families.
- 14% of children lived in poverty.
- 28% were dropping out of school.
- 42% were using alcohol; 14% were using drugs.
- Many children were failing in school, presaging later problems such as school dropout, welfare, or crime.

After considering problems manifest in the schools, analyzing national demographics and issues, and reviewing the local demographics shown above, concerned leaders decided to take action. They established a collaborative project—FANS—in Bryson Middle School. This idea expanded to Woodmont High School as Students Making Alternative Resolutions Together (SMART Team). What did these initiatives look like, and what have they achieved to date?

A mental health adolescent counselor began working a 12-month year at Bryson to provide on-site private clinical therapy to students and families and to coordinate free voluntary counseling on social issues impeding students' adjustment to school and academic achievement. These issues included divorce, stress management, grief, self-esteem and motivation, conflict resolution, and friendship skills. Approximately 33% of Bryson's students volunteered for one or more groups during FANS's first year (1991). Requests for services still outnumber the delivery capacity.

Pluses of FANS

The FANS idea grows with full- or part-time staff in 135 schools in 29 counties statewide through Department of Mental Health state funding with no direct costs to the school districts. Some SC legislators are advocating for general funding to expand replication efforts to support school success by pooling multiagency funds. Even without state funding, some systems are replicating FANS with district funds or through interagency processes. Site-based school services; the absence of a client no-show rate; the availability of Medicaid billing; and the uniting of parents, students, and educators with human service agencies are favorable results that encourage collaborative action.

FANS offers alternatives to incarceration of juvenile offenders. Because people from the Department of Juvenile Justice now work with school and mental health personnel, judges can assign some nonviolent juvenile clients back to schools and their home communities with stipulations for probation and participation in the FANS program. Likewise, the principals can use FANS as an alternative to multiple suspensions or expulsion for students with discipline problems. Students stay in school instead of roaming the streets, and collaborators work to improve student welfare.

An action-research initiative demonstrated FANS's utility as a resource in alleviating stressors of 59 sixth graders at risk of school failure because of truancy, poor grades, discipline problems, or family crises (Hoover, 1992). Twenty high school students and 70 business employees tutored these targeted sixth graders while FANS and school personnel addressed their academic and social problems in small-group sessions. At year's end, FANS results met all specified goals for the group. Similar results occurred the next year. Note a few sample outcomes (Hoover, 1992):

Indicator	FANS (n = 59)	Others (n = 820)
Attendance	95%	96%
GPA	2.1	2.5
In-school suspensions	31[a]	545[a]
Out-of-school suspensions	7[a]	270[a]

a. Duplicated tallies; not individual students.

FANS is cost efficient as well as outcome effective. Direct costs contributed by mental health agencies for FANS were about $44,000 per year. Minimal in-kind costs were absorbed by the school system.

SMART Thinking

A school-community initiative at Woodmont High School, Piedmont, South Carolina is the SMART Team. Woodmont is a rural, community-based school that is experiencing problems often associated with inner-city schooling: busing, social and racial conflicts, some crime and violence, and a general tension of traditional community values pulling against nontraditional trends. SMART addresses student violence and decision-making skills directly.

Personnel from Woodmont High School, the Upstate Mediation Network, and the SC Council for Mediation and Alternative Dispute Resolution work together with endorsement of the SC Bar Association. Local attorneys, members of the Greenville County Solicitor's Office and Sheriff's Department, university professors, psychologists, business partners, church officials, and parents assist Woodmont's efforts in sponsoring one of SC's first high school mediation programs with an officially trained and sanctioned team of peer mediators. Conflict resolution includes mediation between student-teacher, teacher-teacher, teacher-administrator, and parent-school. With the help of people from local churches and businesses, plans include expanding mediation services to community members. Using a modified version of the mediation format and of interagency collaboration, Woodmont has achieved results shown in Table 2.1. Although school enrollments have increased slightly, there have been reductions in suspensions, dropouts, and need for police assistance. There have also been increases in academic recognitions. Interviews show that students, teachers, and parents credit SMART as one contributing effort in the gains.

Programs such as FANS and SMART span multicultural and gender issues because they specifically address shared problems of school and community. Student leaders emerge through expanded opportunities for personal and group expression. Parents express relief that collaborative efforts are focused on student achievement

TABLE 2.1 Some SMART Team Results at Woodmont High
School (1993 and 1994): Students in Grades 9 to 12 (n = 900)

Event	Pre-SMART 1992-1993 (n)	SMART 1993-1994 (n)	Increase or (Reduction) (%)
Suspensions	114	64	(44)
Dropouts	46	12	(74)
Police assistance calls	38	20	(47)
Academic recognitions (3.5 GPA minimum)	81	107	32
Perfect attendance	174	183	5

and that school personnel address emotional and physical welfare
and school safety issues along with emphasis on student academic
growth. State agency personnel view school collaboration as a
means of helping adolescents in proactive—not just reactive—
ways. And public school educators are glad that someone else
cares about kids, too. The increasing burden to be "everyone's
everything" is shared—and the load is not as heavy. These programs have their own goals, which show school success that can
be reported to school critics.

How?

The Big Question

Taking Stock

Many articles express ideas about the "what" issue: that collaboration should be done in schools. Few publications explain how people make successful collaborations happen and how people feel along the way. Seeking "a sense of community" to infiltrate the total educational process does not come naturally to most practitioners, even though most educators say that they need the public's help in meeting the needs of students. Schools have been cells of isolation for so long that many educators do not know how to escape the traditional school structure (Lortie, 1975). Seeking new avenues of support for problems affecting student achievement and for building effective schools can be a personally and professionally threatening undertaking—or it can be an exciting discovery. *Educators must embark on the exploration.*

Issues beyond the school walls now invade—and too often conquer—the once traditional structure of school life. To launch a strategic counterattack, educators need to recruit and train groups of parents, agency personnel, and community leaders who will coalesce to solve problems that were handled previously by other institutions (such as family or religion), that may have been neglected, or that even were hidden by education's high drop-out rates of the past. All parties must converge with unity of purpose that is devoid of "turf tussles." To identify and reduce obstacles to unity, educators will examine closely and challenge aggressively certain issues that present enormous barriers to successful interagency collaboration. Educators need clear and positive answers to new questions:

- Do we really want outside help within our school, or is this being forced upon us?
- *Why* do we want help? (For programs, social issues, student achievement, or community relations?)
- Can we let down our barriers, work through issues of power, and be patient as outsiders learn about the political agendas of schools?
- Can we accept interagency help without being defensive, possessive, and uninviting?
- Are we ready to examine our needs, problems, and weaknesses as one step to promoting stronger schools?
- How many community voices can we hear at once? Do we need to hear only a select few? Which ones?
- Can we share leadership roles to promote more "win-win" situations for students, teachers, and the community?

The Road to Collaboration: The Beginnings

Perhaps a story will help. The explanation of one road taken to achieve collaboration shows the personal and professional issues that accompany serious efforts through collaboration.

I'm a principal* in public schools. As every other principal I know, I work hard to educate students; to make school relevant and enjoyable; make some students' lives more tolerable; and to make school less of a nightmare for children struggling with adult-

*Susan Hoover, a principal in the School District of Greenville County, South Carolina, provides the first-person narrative throughout the text.

type problems: divorce, poverty, pregnancy, substance abuse, crime, violence, esteem, and so on.

After 14 years of teaching, I was a middle school principal (1,200 pupils, Grades 6 to 8) for 6 years. Now I'm a high school principal, and I've learned at least one truth: Kids are kids, no matter what grade. When they have problems, when their lives are in turmoil, school success usually doesn't happen. Learning takes a backseat to frustration, anxiety, bullying, alienation, psychological problems, hormones, and apathy. To make matters worse, these symptoms of school failure are contagious, showing up as student unrest and teacher burnout.

Luckily, as I cast about to find some help for the students, teachers, and me, I stumbled into a collaboration with our local mental health clinic that relieved many stressors in students' lives, in teachers' classrooms, and in the school's daily operations. Families and Neighborhood Schools (FANS) began in 1990 between Piedmont Mental Health Center and Bryson Middle School. Collaboration has again expanded to include various departments of the University of South Carolina, other clinics, a state adolescent psychiatric hospital, and numerous school districts. The out-of-the-ordinary is becoming permanent, but the process is evolutionary.

Job roles and personnel changed over the years, but not the original idea to help students through collaborative programs. The original clinic resource collaborator now coordinates the program on the state level. I went to Woodmont High School (Grades 9 to 12) as principal and modified the FANS design to serve high school students. The FANS work led to the SMART Team, another collaboration effort funded by the MetLife Education Foundation and the Upstate Mediation Network. Personnel from Manpower Development Center (MDC), a nonprofit research and development group, assisted Woodmont educators in starting a peer mediation program, one of the first such programs sanctioned in South Carolina (Smith, Lincoln, & Dodson, 1991). One collaborative program led to another, and more community agencies joined the team. The curriculum expanded to include law-related courses, and organizing "Crime Stoppers" increased the role of student government.

Collaboration: A "Happening"

The going wasn't easy in either collaboration. Each journey was interesting, and both were similar. Learning *how* to collaborate is different from any formal administrative training I had encountered. The truth is this: The exact process that worked for me may not work for another principal in another school or community. I discovered this truth when I discussed with other collaborators the steps and processes they used. Their overall experiences are remarkably similar to mine. *But there isn't one step-by-step recipe to learning the subtleties of collaboration.*

Collaboration is a "happening." It occurs in pieces, with the pieces held together by an almost tangible spirit and determination to do something that works for kids. Cunningham (1990) commented that "collaboration imposes new demands on individual professionals and institutions. New skills are required" (p. 15). He's right. There are both open agendas and hidden agendas for those who collaborate, and formal research results do not teach a practitioner the exact dos and don'ts of either agenda. Here are some tips from the field that helped me.

Open Agenda

Like most tasks and crafts, learning how to collaborate requires skills not easily taught. My skills were acquired through trial and error: try, fail, practice, succeed. Sometimes, intuition was the driving force; it just seemed or felt right. After some introspection, I could list my basic process in a "10 easy steps to collaboration" format. However, the political behaviors to make the process work can be assessed only by participants in their unique communities. The section on the hidden agenda of collaboration includes more ideas about these behaviors.

Ten "Easy" Steps

1. Identify one community resource collaborator for program development. (*Resource collaborators*)
2. Assess school needs for academic achievement. (*Academic support*)

3. Assess present or changing demographics and needed student support programs. (*Environmental scan*)

4. Conduct focus groups with students, parents, teachers and staff, and community and business leaders for planning and acceptance. This step could be done through other processes: surveys, Delphi, Charrette. (*Focus groups*)

5. Check availability of funding through conventional and nonconventional sources. (*Funding*)

6. Develop one or two programs for one grade or for one target student audience. (*Program development*)

7. Include a few teachers at the beginning in program development and implementation. (*Teacher participation*)

8. Specify evaluative procedures. (*Evaluative procedures*)

9. Hold periodic but specific informal evaluative conferences. (*Evaluative conferences*)

10. Evaluate each year's efforts and future plans through focus groups, feedback, data analyses, and in other ways. (*Future planning*)

Table 3.1 on pages 20 and 21 summarizes the action steps to collaboration with examples of the people involved (agents), activities, and aftermath, or expected results. The FANS collaborative is the project analyzed.

Hidden Agenda

Following just the "ten easy steps" to collaboration is partly tongue-in-cheek; the open agenda hides layers of political savvy that principals need to motivate others to unite. The hard part of collaboration is learning the working worlds and turf tussles of other professionals as well as knowing the infrastructures of education, with its nearly terminal timidity in the face of change. Recognizing these undercurrents is often learned the hard way. The path through the hidden-agenda maze is tricky, but knowing how to navigate it will help practitioners avoid hassles later.

1. Choose very carefully the resource agency collaborators, especially the first ones. Ask: "What's In It For Me?"

(WIIFM?) and "What's In It For Them?" (WIIFT?) *Be generous.*

2. Work directly with an agency collaborator who has some political power to make things happen in his or her work world. Don't delegate this project to someone on your staff or relegate it to a functionary in the agency. *Be picky.*

3. Keep things as informal as possible. Talk to your collaborator on the phone, over lunch, while driving places. Avoid a paper chase or memo-sending game. *Be cool.*

4. Avoid excessive meetings and elaborate hierarchies of power and reporting; don't "committee to death" a good thing. Strike a balance of involvement, operations, dissemination, and public relations. *Be active.*

5. "Be soft on people but hard on the problem" (Katz & Lawler, 1993, p. 21). Keep focused on the issues to improve. When internal problems occur (and they will), regroup and keep the peace. *Be user-friendly.*

6. Emphasis results, not wide-scale publicity. Ensure that those who help get praise and recognition. *Be humble.*

7. Especially in the early stages, don't hesitate to change the program approach if it doesn't help students, improve school success, or meet with school and community acceptance. *Be realistic.*

8. Think big, but plan and build consistently and methodically in small stages. This is like Sarason's (1973) idea of building carefully a "core group" that will support, advance, and help formalize the change. *Be idealistic.*

People, Not Programs

A successful collaboration depends upon the personal interactions of the collaborators. There are few rules and no set paradigms for the *what* and *how*. *People* make programs work. Establishing trust and mutual respect is the cornerstone. Risk taking is easier when the principal isn't the only one out on the proverbial limb. School and community collaboration depends on the harmonious "marriage" between the school and at least one agency. The principal

Table 3.1 Ten Easy Steps to School-Community Collaboration

Actions	Agents	Activities	Aftermath
1. Resource collaborators	Mental health department and school personnel	• School-based mental health program from agency personnel • Student counseling	• Students' social detractors addressed • Cost efficient • Teacher support for issues affecting learning
2. Academic support	Mental health counselor, teachers, business leaders	• After-school community tutorials for at-risk students • Homework assistance	• Holistic services for targeted students' group • Improved academic mastery • Community involvement with school
3. Environmental scan	School personnel	• School demographics of discipline, attendance, grades • Student surveys of needs	• Voluntary support groups for social issues, such as divorce, conflict resolution, etc.
4. Focus groups (planning and acceptance)	Collaborators: groups of 10 to 15 each of students, parents, staff, and community leaders	Information dialogues: • "What makes a good day at school for you?" • "Where do you go for help with a personal problem?" • "What is the worst impediment to school success here?"	• Qualitative data for program development • Identification of common concerns, areas of support • Information for designing sources of quantitative data collection

5. *Funding*	Collaborators: community resources	• Restructure available funding • Share grant sources • Identify community funding sources or service deliverers	• Cost effectiveness • More services on-site for school and community
6. *Program development*	Collaborators: focus groups	• Curriculum development of academic support program • Voluntary support groups for social problems of students, parents, teachers	• Cooperative spirit among school audience • Students' social and school needs addressed • Increased school participation • Parental support
7. *Teacher participation*	Collaborators: teachers	• In-school advisory board • Mentors for at-risk students	• Teacher buy-in • Pilot program participants • At-risk program established
8. *Evaluative procedures*	Collaborators: stakeholders	• Student service contract hours • Targeted efforts at specific school improvement • Conflict resolution approaches	• Decrease in discipline offenses and suspensions • Improvement in drop-out rates • Volunteer service hours
9. *Evaluative conferences*	Collaborators: stakeholders	• Formal review of evaluative procedures • Informal continuous assessments	• Action research data from school setting • Flexible program
10. *Future planning*	Mix of original and new participants	• Analysis and evaluation of original data questions	• Qualitative and quantitative evaluations • Audience buy-in response • Program adaptation

and the external resource collaborator need to like or respect each other, feel comfortable around each other, and be secure enough in their positions to discuss their limitations. Both must recognize WIIFM and discuss their expectations openly. The school collaborator should be the principal, the person who represents the school to the neighborhood. "As is the principal, so is the school" is a time-proven adage. The school collaborator is the idea person, the visionary, the "keeper of the philosophy." If the school collaborator is not the principal, the person must be a well-known and respected school representative who has authority to act and some time flexibility to be on call as needed.

The resource collaborator must have political clout or power; however, he or she does not have to be the chief executive officer (CEO). An energetic mental health counselor in a clinic may help a principal establish a site-based program by working the system with agency bosses. The clinic director may not have the time, interest, or skills needed in this type of project but will respond positively to a mid-level agency representative with a well-organized plan that cuts through red tape.

Work informally as much as possible. Busy, productive people prefer project performance to plenteous, plodding meetings that steal not only the actual meeting times but also the time to plan and arrange them. Few would agree that frequent, long, formal committee meetings of a dozen people prompt stakeholder buy-in, enthusiasm, and especially program results. Someone in the school should work directly with the school collaborator—someone (a teacher, parent, even a student or two) who can keep up with paperwork, deadlines, and forms. *Don't meet just to meet.*

Successful collaborations aimed at supporting school success, student achievement, or community services deserve publicity. A word of caution, however: *Keep planning low-key, inform all superiors, and seek their counsel.* If media coverage is needed, avoid premature predictions of program outcomes. Work steadily and quietly; results will publicize your efforts.

At the outset, teachers are often mistrustful of "experts" who have arrived to help. The new ideas and programs should support teachers' efforts to teach. The first response that teachers had when they heard about the FANS idea at Bryson Middle School in 1990 was "What else do we have to do? How much paperwork?" They didn't believe that they had nothing new to do, that FANS personnel would work with students at their request. Once they witnessed the program's successes and the WIIFT, they bought in quickly and enthusiastically.

Funding and Resources

Super planning won't make a program happen without resources. Collaborators need purse strings untied. Various funding sources and resources may be available.

1. Agency positions can be shared or split through state funding sources.
2. Agency personnel can relocate to the school site; the agency pays salary and fringe benefits and meets its business and production agendas more efficiently.
3. The school kicks in its share of the costs by providing space, clients, and so on (in-kind). For FANS, the district converted a storage area into a reception or conference room and a counseling center. The school may also reallocate the time of a paraprofessional or some active volunteers, or may share a professional.
4. Business-education partnerships may fund office expenses; provide equipment; or donate furniture, supplies, or services. In some states, prison industries have excellent and economical programs of furniture production and repair.
5. Funding opportunities exist. Seek school, district, state, federal, and foundation avenues of revenues. Expand beyond traditional programs for sources of funds.

The Road to Collaboration (Continued)

The collaborators started with two women who instantly clicked . . . Linda and me. Then Vicki was added. We three just made it happen with no fuss and no fanfare at first.

S. HOOVER

I'm basically territorial and power possessive. In administration training, I learned that the principal was *the* most important decision maker in the school. Perhaps. But in collaborations, people must agree *up front* that some decisions are territorial and some are communal. Linda, at Piedmont Mental Health, and Vicki, the adolescent counselor for FANS, combined their agendas with mine to serve joint clientele. None of us had ever collaborated before on a project outside of our own work worlds. Midway through the first year, I concluded, "This is harder than I first thought." We circumvented some roadblocks after the fact because at the start, we lacked the experience to foresee problems with agency and district procedures, or to let "sacred cows" graze contentedly. Practitioners should not just decide "OK . . . let's collaborate. I think I'm ready." Collaboration can be a mind game that invigorates and frustrates its partners, and educators have to be prepared.

Readiness for a New Role

Prospective school collaborators might try a diagnostic "gut check" to determine personal and professional readiness for a new and demanding school leadership role. Contemplate these questions:

1. What are the important agendas of my school, students, teachers, community, district power brokers, and so on? Are "school successes" and "student achievement" synonymous or different terms here?
2. Can I handle an assessment by outside audiences of the "state of the school" beyond test scores and drop-out data?
3. Can I survive the initial period (it may seem endless) of focus groups when everyone seems to "NBC" (nag, bother, and complain)?
4. Do I have the patience to ease up on the reins, handle turf tussles, and embrace a leadership style not usually taught in higher education preparation programs?
5. Do I understand the impact of the political pressures in the work worlds of all collaborators: personnel hierarchies, power bases, funding sources, legislative trends?

6. Can I discern from the cacophony of school, district, state and agency voices a symphony of one concern for students?
7. Do I have the interest, time, and energy to retrain teachers to work within a collaborative environment?
8. Can I function effectively emotionally outside of and even isolated from the traditional educational hierarchy? (The "Lone Arranger" in my own system)
9. Do I enjoy—have fun—making something new happen? Do I have a pioneer streak? Am I a risk taker?
10. Will I value the importance of a "win-win" agenda for all collaborators, not just a "win" for my own benefit?

"What's In It For Me?" (WIIFM?)

Altruism aside, school and community collaborations benefit all parties, not just students. Each person will ask, "What's in it for me?" The principal and staff face new challenges but also will enjoy new successes, among which can be these:

1. Opportunities for expanded leadership and new involvement for collaborators and community audiences
2. Increased autonomy and accomplishments for staff
3. Increased parental decision making for students' education and for building confidence in schools
4. Continuous learning and action research opportunities in student services, community involvement, and so on
5. School as a hub for comprehensive services
6. New options for solving traditional school, family, and community problems; for example, juvenile justice or family court scenarios
7. Increased and different options for involving schools with families through student services
8. Direct assistance to teachers with at-risk students
9. Reduction of teacher stressors leading to burnout
10. Students' view of school as a caring, positive place
11. New avenues for student decision making and parent involvement

Community residents, and especially parents, will soon see value in collaborative programs. Some outsiders already view the school as *the* disseminating agency of information and services to students. Most will readily accept a holistic service model on campus as part of the educational package, even though they might disagree with one particular program. Parents invited to school for a discipline or academic conference may turn to school personnel for help with a child who is defiant, addicted, or emotionally withdrawn. Consider the difference in hearing from a school employee: (a) the range of on-site help programs for the defiant or troubled student, or (b) "We're so sorry, but that's your family problem. We must discipline your child for disrespect of the teacher." The first option offers a supportive choice that addresses the problem and cements good school-community relations. The second option is cold and bureaucratic. The first option allows students to benefit from collaborative programs in ways beyond direct services. They gain trust in school personnel and confidence in their school. In summary, "WIIFM" translates to one word: "Lots."

"What's In It For Them?" (WIIFT)

Sometimes when I walked into the school, I felt like a piece of Velcro . . . students and problems clinging to me.

LINDA SMITH, Piedmont Mental Health Center

The initial FANS collaboration wasn't easy, but the Piedmont Mental Health Center resource collaborator had positional authority and the backing of a local supervisor and the state mental health commissioner to deliver services to troubled adolescents in a different and more effective model than the traditional center-based approach. They wanted to test new service delivery models, increase client services, and save money and time. They wanted to do more with less—a familiar tune.

Linda Smith secured a federal start-up grant through the supportive efforts of Dr. Gary Melton, Director of the Families in Society Program of the University of South Carolina. She then contacted personnel of the Greenville County School District, and eventually I joined the project. The collaboration started with two women who instantly clicked . . . Linda and me. Then Vicki Fanning, the adolescent counselor, was added. We three just made the program work through common goals, compatible work habits, mutual respect . . . and, whether anyone else believes it, through intuition of what would and wouldn't work in the school and community.

Among the WIIFT benefits of the FANS collaboration for the mental health program were

1. Increased adolescent services to include more direct counseling and indirect client and school services (volunteer groups)
2. Dramatic decreases in no-shows for appointments (student clients seen during school day), from approximately 50% to about 10%
3. Parental satisfaction with the direct communication between school and outside agency personnel in working with student problems
4. Medicaid third-party billing for affordable student services
5. School employee acceptance of unified school and mental health services as part of the school's total service mix
6. Research opportunities in site-based delivery services
7. Expansion of agency collaboration for total case management
8. Efficient fund pooling and personnel sharing
9. Opportunities for nontraditional counseling in schools
10. Support services for effective parenting
11. Mental health information to an expanded community audience
12. Consistent follow-up contacts between counselor and clients at school
13. Structured intake referral processes and follow-up for emergency student problems requiring restrictive help (e.g., hospitalization)

How to Be an Agency Resource Collaborator

In a school-based collaboration with outside agencies, educators have the home-court advantage; they probably have to do less adjusting than do the agency resource collaborators. In a "foreign world" of constantly clanging bells, hordes of frantically stirring people, and a unique web of spinning political threads, resource collaborators are the minority members of school-based partnerships. They must gain personal and professional acceptance by faculty, students, parents, and community members. Some strategies and advice to ease this transition are the following:

1. Gain trust—slowly but surely—by "walking the talk."
2. Be visible at school in hallways, the cafeteria, break areas, homerooms, classrooms, bus loading areas, and at school activities—to be perceived as part of the "real school."
3. Decisions are not just top down. Even if the collaborators are the "experts," keep the teachers and parents involved in program planning, implementing, and evaluating.
4. Pull a few rabbits out of the hat right away. Be an immediate, positive addition to the school family. Let news of positive results spread informally throughout the school and community. Word of mouth has tremendous power!
5. Learn the hierarchy or the hidden agenda in the school, and link up with some movers and shakers. Provide frequent, informal feedback of program development and results.
6. Be a positive factor in the school, but be ready for some negative responses from internal and external saboteurs.
7. Relieve school staff of program paperwork.
8. Assist the principal with an action research project supporting students and benefiting school and agency agendas.
9. Gain some knowledge of effective schools research and applicable educational programs.
10. Make today's "unheard of and impossible" tomorrow's "been there and done that!" Be a change agent.

Damage Control Plan

It happens. Collaboration breaks down sometimes. Externally, political forces or warring groups opposed to one program may try to shut down all activities or deny funding. Internally, you may face bickering, turf tussles, or neglected job responsibilities. Fix the flat tire so the car can move along.

Collaborative programs usually deal with sensitive issues that some believe are out of the school's domain. Opposition can become combative. To counter external opposition, the collaborators need data to support how well (quality) and how much (quantity) the program benefits the school and the community. Quantitative information is helpful, especially data about suspensions, dropouts, truancy, test scores, agency interventions, and so on. Opinions count, too. Keep anecdotes and client comments for public relations purposes and for program planning. Keep records of new or unusual options that the collaboration allows: new arrangements for family or juvenile court, classroom teaching opportunities for the sheriff's department, and so on.

Deal with opposition quietly, but firmly and quickly. Inform supervisors of problems. Have some preestablished indicators of high concern over the program. In other words, are these complaints "normal crazy" or "crazy crazy"? What events trigger real concern? Have a network of community support people ready to deflect attacks and repair damages.

Internally, school staff may feel threatened by the introduction of new personnel or programs. They may infer that school or student achievement problems are perceived to be their fault because new people are now on campus "to fix things." Lack of understanding or frustration can abet sabotaging. Passive (even active) aggression may be directed against the resource collaborator, the principal, the program, or all three. People frustrated about change usually react . . . often negatively.

How to sell—or perhaps resell—a disenchanted faculty on a nontraditional approach to holistic school services begins by educating them on the big demographic profile of American youth and their social problems. Next, teacher groups might analyze the same demographic indicators of need for students at the school, or in the county if localized school data are not available. Collaborators might engage teachers in focus groups to assess their levels of frustration, anxiety, interest, and support. These sessions need to occur regularly, even unofficially veiled as program feedback, to keep the collaboration afloat. Collaborators must continue to educate the educators on the needs of the program.

A damage control plan is important because collaborators operate in different political worlds. Resource collaborators may not fully understand how one parental complaint, seemingly minor, can quickly spark a wildfire at school. School collaborators may not fully understand client confidentiality required by agency personnel. All parties need to be ready when the moment arrives to address concerns, enlist support, or modify the program.

Handling Problems

When problems occur within the collaboration, things get personal; barriers go up and results suffer. One incident is a good example of a bad situation.

In an altercation, a high school student who was tutoring a sixth grader in an after-school FANS program grabbed the neck of the sixth grader in an aggressive, choking manner. Mental health personnel intervened and contacted the sixth grader's mother, but neither the high school principal of the tutor nor I was immediately informed of the matter.

When we two principals and our supervisor did learn of the incident, we objected to being isolated from knowledge of the problem. We wanted to impose stronger disciplinary action than the mental health staff had initiated. The collaborators got into a heated hassle. Mental health personnel saw the incident as a "bump" to smooth out; school officials saw it as a serious problem with legal implications of student supervision. Much talking and little listening were happening.

I initially wanted the high school student suspended from school and removed from the program. Linda wasn't overly concerned about school discipline; she focused on understanding how the screening process to identify tutors could be improved. I was concerned that the sixth grader's parent would demand legal recourse or cause major waves for the program with my superiors. Fortunately, the problem was far less serious than we first thought. The sixth grader was not hurt, and the parent was never overly concerned. The issue was resolved with a suspension for the high school tutor, whom we kept in the program. We reviewed carefully all guidelines for future tutor screening.

In working through the problem, we learned much about active listening skills and about each other's political work worlds. We agreed to disagree—if the need arose again—within guidelines. Using active listening strategies is not easy. We had to get past the emotional issues of power, control, and ego before we could process content. Only then did we realize that we shared common beliefs about the seriousness of the incident and concern over student and program welfare. In active listening, both the emotional and the factual parts must be heard and processed before there is movement toward resolution. We learned this lesson the hard way.

This important incident was the turning point for Linda to recognize the complexities and repercussions inherent in discipline problems, parents' perceptions, school liability, and public relations. I better understood the mental health agenda and the sincerity of the mental health personnel in helping people through rough spots. Both of us gained trust for each other's professional competency.

Pitfalls of Collaboration

So, collaboration is supposed to be great. You've tried the tips, identified your goals, fought off the opposition, but things just aren't clicking; nothing's really happening. The "collaboration" is a power struggle, a hassle. Pitfalls await unwary practitioners. Certain contingencies within the business and school worlds have enormous influences on the ease of a principal's efforts. Here are troublesome areas in forming collaboratives:

1. The resource agency staff probably isn't used to collaborating with "foreigners" either. They may not know how to

share leadership roles, responsibilities, or problems. Everyone is trying to maintain his or her separate roles in traditional ways but in the guise of teamwork: the "same but different, together but separate" facade.

2. A good clue of an encroaching problem is the paper trail. When people stop talking and rely only on reading memos from each other, human interaction is lost. The sharpness of the original reason for collaboration can dull and become just one more nebulous item to complete, check off, and say, "We did that. It didn't work." One critical step in developing successful collaboration is establishing and maintaining joint ownership for a win-win agenda. *Communicate.*

3. In an age of bottom-line accountability, failure to produce is hyped by negative media exposure. The political climate for risk taking in education is oppressive in many locales. Principals are expected not to rock the boat. Veering from safe, well-known channels to explore new seas may not be rewarded unless the program is data driven.

4. Equally frustrating is a district climate that squelches risk taking. Principals are responsible for their leadership decisions, no argument. Conversely, a certain amount of resources, moral and financial support, and upper management commitment must accompany a principal's ventures into collaborative program models. The process is too involved to be successful without upper-level support. Only a rare person will voluntarily risk a job on a long-term collaborative investment when only short-term returns are demanded.

5. Few people understand the emotional stress that most principals undergo as they try to do more and more with the proverbial less and less. Collaboration is, indeed, a "more and more" approach, but when correctly established, it ultimately uses less and less in the commodities of time, energy, and stress. In the beginning, collaborating can cause frustration, anxiety, and anger. *Be patient.*

6. Collaboratives can't just be "feel good" programs. Do your homework thoroughly and be a visionary. Know the school and community demographics; analyze test scores, student behavior, and attendance patterns; and identify student needs. Communicate this information.

Working through pitfalls requires faith in one's own abilities and a penchant for doing the right thing. *Collaboration* is a buzz word that some educators might believe will pass like so many other previously hot topics. But frankly, school folks have long collaborated in some form: with clergy, parents, civic clubs, each other, and so on. Two main differences now are that collaboration provides economic as well as programmatic benefits, and that it's not just a fad with high visibility. In transformational leadership, principals lead through "vision" and getting consensus on a "common vision." According to Seeley, Niemeyer, and Greenspan (1991), collaboration in the 1990s is a process series of actions, when being "'visionary' becomes practical and necessary" (p. 28).

Who?

Educators and Caregivers

Common Threads of Collaboratives

Creative educators and caregivers collaborate because of their joint concern for people. Meeting students' human service needs and educating them in a productive environment are difficult goals to achieve in piecemeal fashion under the best of circumstances. Although some states now mandate school and community collaborations, these collaboratives won't survive unless they have a common thread: A sincerity to improve services. The following are summaries of but a few programs nationwide exhibiting sincere purpose, solid planning, and support.

Comer School Improvement Process in Dade County, Florida

A large-scale, national collaborative effort is the Comer School Improvement Process. An operating example is Dade County's Fienberg-Fisher Elementary School. This full-service community school has both a mission statement for educators and one for service providers of the Miami Beach community. The core of the program includes (a) about a dozen parent's programs to involve parents at every level of school activity, (b) a school management team (SMT) to plan and coordinate school activities, (c) home-school services that emphasize prevention and family preservation and management of individual cases, (d) a school improvement team (SIT) that systematically addresses academic achievement and social climate and public relations goals, (e) staff development needs created by the school's mission and goals, and (f) assessment and modification (Fienberg-Fisher Elementary School, n.d.).

The Miami Herald ("Beyond the Three R's," 1993) reported that full-service schools resulted from collaborative delivery of education, medicine, and social or human services to help remove barriers to student learning. The Dade County schools have received considerable grant support from private and public sources for setting up full-service schools.

The Pioneers, Biggs Early Childhood Center, Covington, Kentucky

This half-day program serves approximately 300 at-risk 4-year-olds in collaboration with United Way. Parenting skills are emphasized in a specific course and applied during voluntary and paid services (Hochberg & Lopez, 1993).

The Center, Leadville, Colorado

Using family counseling assistance programs and social services agencies for income, food, and health concerns, The Center addresses needs from preschoolers to senior citizens. Teenage pregnancy, effective parenting, special education needs, and adult education are targets of services. Notably, the local school district provides only the building and contributes to The Center's governance (Hochberg & Lopez, 1993).

Family Services Center, Gainesville, Florida

School-based services address health, education, social services, and family support. Specifically identified needs of at-risk elementary and middle school students are the focus (Hochberg & Lopez, 1993).

Family and Neighborhood Services (FANS),
Greenville, South Carolina

The state's first school-based mental health service project started in a middle school in 1990. This model now serves students and communities in more than 135 sites in 29 counties statewide. Mental health personnel as well as doctoral interns in educational administration, counseling, and social work support the joint educational and social needs of students, families, and communities. Traditional clinical counseling, voluntary student support groups, classroom assistance, and community programs address issues related to teenage pregnancy, parenting, special education, tutoring and study skills, community support programs, and juvenile justice concerns (Hoover & Achilles, 1995).

New Beginnings Center for Children and Families,
San Diego, California

School-based in portable classrooms on an elementary school campus, New Beginnings was one of the founders of the current school and community collaborative movement. The program is aimed at combating the negative forces of street gang violence, family poverty, women and children's physical victimization, and decay and diversity in the inner city. The center is a joint venture of San Diego schools and the departments of health, social service agencies, city government, University of California Medical School, Children's Hospital, and various community service organizations (Payzant, 1992). Promoting family self-sufficiency and conducting extensive home visits are preludes to a smooth transition to schooling (Busse & Jehl, 1994).

Common Denominators

Each collaborative program model has unique elements, but all share several key elements. These denominators lead the collaborators down successful "how-to" paths.

1. Programs are on the school campus or adjacent to it. Community members can transfer the trust associated with a

local school to a new program. Site-based or family models do more than "fix" social ills. Preventive, proactive programs for all children, birth through adolescence, address school and social needs. Adults' needs may be addressed in ESL and parenting skills classes, GED programs, and so on.

2. Someone has to be in charge. Paid staffs are preferable to volunteers. However, if volunteers are the total staff, appoint a coordinator.

3. Most programs include components of social services and/or mental health that will support education efforts.

4. All program services and components link to ultimate school success of the students: tutoring, classroom support, special education needs, teacher training, parent involvement, and so on.

5. Teachers respect the program and support the school's involvement in the collaboration.

6. The program leaders communicate their service models to the public in appropriate and timely ways.

7. Collaborators respect each other's separate roles and joint contributions, and they plan to share strengths.

8. Program leaders seek different and creative funding sources: grants, joint co-pay, service bartering, and so on.

9. Programs are fluid; they shift and change when needs do.

10. Family involvement in the welfare of children is paramount.

In an age of parental noninvolvement in schools, collaborative programs declare that schools are user- and family-friendly places. They link school, community, and family by offering visible support to children. Parents are actively involved partners, tools for building community collaborations, and decision makers in their children's education (Cochran, 1993, p. 40). School and community collaborative programs are "a direct signal from the school to parents that they are welcome in the building to engage in collaboration in the education of their children" (Johnson, 1994, p. 42). Collaborative programs give parents hope for their children and their children's futures.

All students, too, can directly participate in school, even the at-risk ones. In school-based collaborations, the ultimate goal is educational success. Families appreciate the extended services that help their children have better chances for success in school. This appreciation transfers to school engagement. One student not dropping out of school is a success to be counted, and "success for all reinforces the partnership concept" (Seeley et al., 1991, p. 29).

Collaboratives: Cooperative or Coerced?

Problems within our social structure, street mayhem encroaching on school property, tighter and shorter purse strings for education, a heightened sense of business and education's joint responsibility for America's children—whatever the reason, collaboratives are now being touted as effective, efficient, and morally right in meeting basic human needs and in providing a nurturing foundation for education. Recognizing the school and community benefits of collaboratives, some states are legislating or mandating joint agency ventures. Although many mandates take form as early childhood or family programs, states have not limited the options. School personnel are encouraged—directed, in some cases—to develop collaboratives to address all types of educational needs.

Two State Statutes

Recent legislation from two states shows how policy and legislation are urging collaborative action. The two states and the years of their legislation are South Carolina (1993) and Delaware (1994). The comments about South Carolina's Act 135 (Early Childhood Development and Academic Assistance Act, 1993) are excerpted from the School Improvement Council Assistance's publication *SICA News.*

South Carolina broke new grounds for school autonomy and student success with the 1993 passage of the Early Childhood Development and Academic Assistance Act (Act 135). Act 135 redirects over $95 million from the nationally acclaimed Education Improvement Act (EIA) to permit districts, schools, and teachers to determine how best to promote student success.

The legislation allows flexibility to provide services for any student, not just those determined "at risk"; . . . Act 135 has two main divisions. One is to focus on early childhood development and prevention of academic difficulties so that students are on track by grade three. Also inherent in this section of the act is the development of a parenting and family literacy program. . . . *Collaboration* [italics added] among education, social service agencies, and adult education coordinates the offerings of this parenting component.

The second division of Act 135 is the academic assistance component for grades 4-12. These main divisions have two consistent threads: staff development opportunities for Act 135 strategies and newly *emerging on-going relationships between school and community resources. Health, social, and mental health agencies, families, business, communities, and schools unite to pool resources to conquer impediments to students' school success* [italics added].

School districts and local school personnel, parents, and community leaders develop Five-Year Plans to address the appropriate components of Act 135. (*SICA News*, 1994, passim)

South Carolina received national recognition in the early 1980s for its acclaimed Educational Improvement Act (EIA), which was designed primarily to attack deficiencies in skill mastery. South Carolina educators and community residents have also recognized that learning occurs in and outside the school building. The new Act 135 legislation supports basic skills mastery with an additional component addressing family support.

Act 135 goes beyond traditional scope in seeking answers. It mandates school and community collaboration as part of the solution to the tidal wave of student needs washing over the schools. The legislation includes required parenting/family literacy for early childhood support, and the "innovative initiative" addresses children's various social and educational needs in K-12 settings. Act 135 charges educational service deliverers to create

appropriate relationships between school and other social service agencies by improving relationships between the school and community agencies (health, social, mental health), parents and the business community, and by reestablishing procedures that cooperatively focus the resources of the greater community upon barriers to success in school, particularly in the areas of early childhood and parenting programs, after-school programs, and adolescent services. (Early Childhood Development and Academic Assistance Act, 1995, Section II)

The State Superintendent of Education and the Commissioner for Higher Education founded the South Carolina Council on Education Collaboration (SCCEC) in 1991. BellSouth provided SCCEC with funding to accomplish several goals, notably collaborating with the South Carolina Chamber of Commerce on workforce competencies in the curriculum frameworks and serving as a catalyst for statewide innovation. The council oversees collaborative efforts affecting K-12 students, assists with all levels of project funding, and functions as a resource for other states desiring the "hows" of collaboration (SCCEC, 1994).

The State of Delaware has also developed legislation to support collaborative solutions to school and social problems. The following information about a Delaware initiative is excerpted from the *Regulations Governing Alternative, Intervention and Prevention Programs* (Delaware State Board of Education, 1994) and the Delaware Department of Public Instruction, Implementation Grants for Family Support System, State of Delaware Family Services Cabinet Council (1994) report titled *Collaboration*. In Delaware, House Bill (HB) 247 was passed in June 1994 and signed into law in July, 1994. HB 247 authorizes three types of programs. *Two of the three relate to collaboration on student service delivery* [italics added]: a) school district/school-based intervention programs and b) community based/school-linked prevention programs for students and families. The introduction to the draft guidelines states:

> Because schools are the reflection of the total community, the total community must assume responsibility for providing resources toward this effort. Such resources can be provided by the Department of Services for Children, Youth and Families; by the Department of Health and Social Services; by community based, and private agencies . . . [and] the Department of Public Instruction and the . . . local school districts. (Delaware State Board of Education, 1994, p. 1)

The draft guidelines for preparing proposals (Delaware Department of Public Instruction, 1994) notes that "school districts must be the primary applicant" for service delivery that take a coordinated approach (collaboration among agencies) that may include "multi-agency service plans and unitary case management." These collaborations will, among other things, "provide support to schools and families that will improve the school climate for learning" through integrated delivery systems. All applications must "involve a minimum of one school district, local government agency and community organization who agree to provide coordinated family services and commit resources" (passim).

These statutes from two states demonstrate the serious concern of policy persons in trying formal collaborative efforts to help solve community problems that spill over into schools and detract from education goals. State initiatives may be extensions of the federal Family Support Act (FSA) of 1988. The laws provide directions for agency persons to establish the formal collaborations that many people believe can activate the "less is more" idea that seems popular today with politicians.

In the KISS (Keep It Simple Somehow) spirit, a low-key collaborative demonstrates the power of the individual in establishing the process. Jackie Robinson, principal of Stubbs Elementary School (Grades 4 to 6) in Wilmington, Delaware, described a collaborative effort that predates the state legislative activity (personal communication, November 1994). This individual-oriented project embodies the idea that collaborative activity is low key, person directed, and student oriented. The "success committee" is the heart of this collaborative.

Anyone (teacher, counselor, parent, etc.) can initiate a "success committee" for an at-risk student. Each committee includes at least the principal, counselor, nurse, and student's teacher. Each committee works with its one student client to bring into the equation whatever resources will help the student succeed. The nurse serves as a link to health and mental health services; the assistant principal and counselor help with in-school behavior; and the principal links to a group that Jackie calls "community friends." She formed this group when she realized that the school alone could not cope with school failure, indiscipline, and community issues. She sought help. The "community friends" provided direct help (e.g., tutors or just listening to kids read) and also offered information about other sources of support. The program gets no extra money, although the principal's supervisor attends meetings and helps where he can, such as by disseminating results of the project's successes. The supervisor's interest and attendance provide an "official stamp" of legitimation for this project.

The principal wants the project to continue on this informal basis and notes that if money is taken from other sources, that money often brings constraints that could hinder project operation. Jackie says, "Because we don't know in advance what the kids will need and what we need to do to help them, it's hard to specify in advance in a proposal what it is we are going to do. Thus, we need much leeway, and a source of outside funds would probably require us to specify in advance the use of those funds."

No *formal* data are being compiled to assess this program, but the success committees in 1 year numbered about 60 in January, and by June, only 15 were still necessary. This means that 45 of the 60 youngsters had worked themselves out of trouble, and the committees had worked themselves out of jobs. The 15 or so youngsters still working with success committees were recommended for summer school or other intervention. When the school has no retention in grade, the principal gives much of the credit for this success to interventions of the success committees and community friends.

This vignette emphasizes that there is no single answer to what collaborators can do, how they work, and who is involved. Successful collaboratives seem to fit the vagaries of their unique contexts. Jackie's story shows most of the key elements that drive collaborative successes: low key, individual energy, sharing, concern, reasonable and not restrictive structure, upper-level support, and a spirit of community. If nothing else, collaborating for student success adds opportunities for students and their parents or guardians to get reconnected to schools and to participate in a school-related activity that is designed to help them succeed. There are strong research-based reasons for activities that offer added opportunities for student engagement in school.

Finn (1989) reviewed available research and found that student participation in school increased student identification with school and reduced the incidence of later dropout. This finding has been echoed by Elias and Srebnik (1993). Finn and Cox (1992) found that students in small classes of about 15 students (thus with increased opportunities for participation) had greater positive school participation than did students in larger classes (e.g., about 25 students). Added services at the school site increase the potential for student participation in school and school-related events. These findings should not be surprising when contemplated along with the considerable evidence of the deleterious effects of large schools on student achievement and behavior (e.g., Fowler & Walberg, 1991). Collaboration provides one way to add a caring and service dimension to the school mission and to "demassify" second-wave, assembly-line schools (Toffler & Toffler, 1995).

The emphasis on collaboration has implications for education preparation programs, professional development, action research, and other trends in education. One way to encourage collaboration is to fold as many of the previously mentioned ideas into regular education programming as makes sense. Chapter 5 suggests some ways to get started.

When and Where

"When Do I Know, and Where Do I Go?"

Although there are now federal laws (e.g., Family Support Act) and state statutes (e.g., Delaware, South Carolina) supporting collaboration, the many "C" words regaining currency are not new in education (cooperation, community, collaboration, councils, compromise, co-optation, compact, etc.). There have been regional cooperatives, community education, business-education compacts, boards of cooperative services, and study councils. What is new at this time are (a) popularization of the word *collaboration*, (b) the politics and media attention, (c) the social and economic contexts, and (d) some of the structures and arrangements. Political agendas, downsizing of bureaucracy, client service models, and the Orwellian idea that "less is more" impel the sharing of resources, facilities, and clients. Times and methods are changing.

Laying the Groundwork for Success

The fairly sudden shift from institutional autonomy to seeking mutually beneficial ways to increase the impact of the work by cooperating with multiple agencies brings with it the desire to learn how to collaborate effectively. Traditional preparation programs for people seeking roles in education will need time to get geared up to be of much help: The skills now needed are not learned in lecture halls, and little research and evaluation have been done to provide a definitive knowledge base on collaboration. There is little information to guide people who are seeking ways to build collaborative efforts other than reports of practice and the anecdotal stories of interesting successes. Some well-publicized national initiatives are beginning to offer data of success. Information and ideas are also available from people who conduct activities that support, but are tangential to, collaboration as described here.

Putting Out the Welcome Mat

If educators want schools to become the hub of human services delivery, the schools must be *inviting places.* Invitational theory is useful here in helping educators to make schools inviting and safe places. There are many sources of ideas about invitational theory, but a good place to start is with Purkey (1992), who notes that places can be intentionally or unintentionally *disinviting,* or they can be unintentionally or intentionally *inviting.* Educators can move the school toward being an intentionally inviting environment by attending carefully to people, policies, programs, processes, and places. Don't leave things to chance. Emphasis on community helps set the stage for collaboration (e.g., Etzioni, 1993; Oakes and Quartz, 1995). The push for "school-to-work" initiatives and for service learning is drawing advocates and researchers. These phenomena are part of the social context that is facilitating collaboration and extending the earlier business-education partnership movement.

Learning Collaboration Skills

Skills related to diversity and the need to work with multiple constituencies to achieve a shared vision or common ground (e.g., Yankelovich, 1991) will help the educator who is struggling with collaboration. The skills needed to start and/or collaborate successfully may have some overlap with what is taught in traditional education preparation programs, but mostly the skills are more art than science and thus have not been previously a serious part of the higher education agenda: group process, agenda setting, negotiations, nonverbal communication, nonjargon writing, consensus building, community analysis, focus groups, compromise, seeking common ground, and making connections. Some necessary personal attributes for building collaboration may never be part of a graduate program: humility, common sense, caring, entrepreneurship, risk taking, political acumen, activism. Much of what needs to be learned will be trial-and-error methods on site (on-the-job training, or OJT).

Encouraging Faculty Involvement

As part of planned, continuing professional development, leaders of the collaborative should invite faculty members to become involved, if only in helping to track, evaluate, and disseminate the results of the collaborative activity. Two of Sparks and Loucks-Horsley's (1989) five models of staff development (inquiry and involvement in a developmental activity) may be used effectively as part of a faculty's continuing growth plan and in actually operating a collaborative. Faculty members at the site can participate in the collaborative and can help conduct research and evaluation as part of their personalized inservice growth programs. In the spirit of collaboration, faculty who are graduate students in courses for credit may even work with their university faculty to plan and conduct research and evaluation activities in the schools and to help disseminate information through articles and other materials for distribution (Knapp, 1995; Stallings, 1995). Results of well-done research should find their way into higher education curricula so that people in preparation for either school roles or other agency work can learn about the benefits and the results of collaborative activity. But, of course, there is more. Faculty should be involved directly in making the school an inviting place, delivering services to the clients, and coordinating with the cooperating agencies.

Sharing Collaborative Responsibilities

The intense interest in collaboration is partially driven by the increasing difficulty of the education task (see Cooley, 1993) and the need to get on with schooling (see Stallings, 1995). The economic pressure for both parents to work (*if* there are two parents) has contributed to the decline of the traditional family role. *In loco parentis* is taking on new meaning, as Heath and McLaughlin (1991) reported:

> Though the school may extend its family-like relationships by including within its perimeter a variety of social agencies, it is hardly a substitute for the family of yesteryear. Then the family was the nucleus of all social activity and direction giver of its youth. However, in society today, too many families simply lack the emotional, financial, or cognitive supports that a developing youngster requires. (p. 624)

At least for now, collaboration seems to be a reasonable grass-roots approach to help educators share problems and solutions with caregivers in other agencies of society. As collaboration becomes popular, it surely will be studied to death by academicians, who will then offer that the models, processes, and typologies based upon their research constitute the "correct" way to get the job done. We know of no surer way to kill the thrill of finding unique ways to collaborate to improve the condition of people and to advance the goals of education than to subject collaboratives to endless evaluations and studies that surely will offer prescriptions. In this endeavor, we hope that the practitioners will accept the leadership, employ sound action research steps, and invite the academics to collaborate with *them!*

Roadmap to the Future

Although the national data and studies are harbingers to initiate concern, the changes and collaboration will occur school by school. In the best of school restructuring and site-based management, local educators and citizens must review their own data, conditions, and goals for education as they begin to employ collaborative school-community services. *Local leaders must know and act upon their own demographic data. If good data are not available and useful, start now to change that.*

In discussing the need to change education administrator preparation and the need for administrators to attend to new roles, Cunningham (1990) noted that "collaboration between and among agencies serving children and youth promises to be a prominent part of the work of educational leaders in the future" (p. 14). "More recently, federal policy has demanded collaboration for agencies to qualify for federal monies (e.g., the Family Support Act [FSA] of 1988). FSA forces collaboration at state and local levels. . . . A new vocabulary is emerging" (p. 15). Some state statutes encourage collaboration. It is heartening that policymakers and legislators are helping educators move into this important area of school improvement.

Annotated Bibliography
and References

Annotated Bibliography

The annotated bibliography is categorized according to the practitioner's needs in the collaborative process: background information, some "how-to" ideas, and program models. Many of the "how-to" references also include descriptions of successful collaborative models.

Background Information on School and Community Collaboration

Curcio, J. L., & First, P. F. (1993). *Violence in the schools: How to practically prevent and defuse it.* Newbury Park, CA: Corwin.

A section of this book reports that the full-service school aids in defusing the effects of gangs and violence. Social programs addressing at-risk descriptors are highlighted: teenage pregnancy, weapons, health needs, poverty, and so on.

Herman, J. L., & Herman, J. J. (Eds). (1994). *People and Education, 2(3).* Thousand Oaks, CA: Corwin.

Two articles in the volume, one by Danzig and one by Wanat et al., deal with the difficulty of uniting parents and educators. The authors contend that understanding the associated social stigma of the under-educated and nonparticipating would assist the collaborative process.

"How-To" Process of School and Community Collaboration

America's Agenda: Schools for the 21st century. (1995, Spring). The activist approach. New York: Scholastic, Inc.

This entire journal issue focuses on parental demands for schools to either assume more roles in their children's lives or relinquish what some parents believe is too much control. For the purpose of the collaborative process, the journal reports on the expanded role that parents need to play in education to form school-parent ties.

Carroll, S. R., & Carroll, D. (1994). *How smart schools get and keep community support.* Bloomington, IN: National Educational Service.

The authors give excellent tips on how schools can gain public confidence and support and how they can market their special programs. How to analyze the community demographics, develop parental involvement, and use public relations tools available to schools are major topics. This book is a good foundation source for educators readying their school audiences for collaborative efforts.

Hammiller, R. E. (1994, October). *The principal's perspective of the possibilities and constraints of neighborhood-based interagency collaboration.* Paper presented at the meeting of the University Council for Educational Administration, Philadelphia.

This paper reports the results of an 18-month study of eight schools in two cities with school and community interagency collaborations based in their neighborhoods, not in the schools. The importance of the principal's role in the schools in making collaboration successful is highlighted. Principals reveal their positive opinions of empowering people in neighborhoods to work collaboratively with schools for effective education.

Kadel, S. (1993). *Interagency collaboration: Improving the delivery of services to children and families.* Greensboro, NC: SouthEastern Regional Vision for Education.

This is an excellent guide to collaboration for practitioners. The "ABC's of Collaboration" is especially helpful, as is the section on creating a family center. The book contains sidebars that feature "Dynamic Ideas," highlights of successful programs, and tips used in schools nationally. Pro-reader, the SouthEastern Regional Vision for Education provides a feedback critique sheet on the book and a form on which to submit other Dynamic Ideas.

Smith, R. C., Lincoln, C. A., & Dodson, D. L. (Eds). (1991). *Let's do it our way: Working together for educational excellence.* Chapel Hill, NC: MDC. *An excellent resource, this book directs a practitioner in the process of uniting school and community audiences for the improvement of schools. The change process of a collaborative effort is labeled "moving vision to action." Useful and informative, this book offers many tips on various planning processes and group dynamics.*

Successful School and Community Collaborative Program Models

Epstein, J. L. (1995). School/family/community partnerships: Caring for the children we share. *Phi Delta Kappan, 76*(9), 701-712. *An excellent framework of six types of involvement carry the reader from the planning stages of collaboration through anticipated results. Epstein strongly advocates community collaboration and parent participation as demonstration of a school restructured in attitude and practice.*

MaWhinney, H. B. (1994, April). *Three frames of leadership in opening the high school door to community collaboration.* Paper presented at the meeting of the American Education Research Association, New Orleans. *MaWhinney describes three high school collaboratives recognized as exemplary by government policy advisors of Ontario, Canada. Structures, strategies, and leadership dimensions needed for success are the focus.*

References

American Association of School Administrators (1995). *Leadership news.* Arlington, VA: Author.

Arthur, G., & Bauman, P. (1994). School-based community services: A study of public agency partnerships. *Journal of School Leadership, 4*(6), 649-671.

Barnett, B. G. (1995). Visioning for the future: What can educational leaders do to build a shared commitment to interagency collaboration. *Journal of School Leadership, 5*(1), 69-86.

Beyond the three R's. (1993, December 8). *The Miami Herald,* p. 18A.

Busse, C., & Jehl, J. (1994). New beginnings for children and families. *Thrust for Educational Leadership, 24*(3), 18-19.

Cochran, M. (1993). Parent empowerment and parent-teacher action research: A friendly critique. *Equity and Choice, 10*(1), 36-40.

Cooley, W. W. (1993). *The difficulty of the educational task.* Pittsburgh: University of Pittsburgh, Pennsylvania Educational Policy Studies (PEPS).

Cunningham, L. L. (1990). Educational leadership and administration: Retrospective and prospective views. In D. E. Mitchell & L. L. Cunningham (Eds.), *Educational leadership and changing contexts of families, communities, and schools* (NSSE 89th Yearbook, Part 2, pp. 1-18). Chicago: University of Chicago Press.

Delaware Department of Public Instruction, Implementation Grants for Family Support System, State of Delaware Family Services Cabinet Council (1994). *Collaboration.* Dover: Author.

Delaware State Board of Education. (1994, February). *Comprehensive school discipline improvement: Regulations governing alternative, intervention and prevention programs* (Draft). Dover: Author.

Early Childhood Development and Academic Assistance Act (Act 135). (1993). Columbia: South Carolina Senate Education Committee.

Elias, M. J., & Srebnik, D. S. (1993). Let's prevent dropout—and other problem behaviors—by fostering engagement in school. *People and Education, 1*(2), 184-195.

Etzioni, A. (1993). *The spirit of community.* New York: Crown.

Fienberg-Fisher Elementary School. (n.d.). *The Fienberg-Fisher full-service community school* (Brochure). 1420 Washington Ave., Miami Beach, FL 33139.

Finn, J. D. (1989). Withdrawing from school. *Review of Educational Research, 59*(5), 117-142.

Finn, J. D., & Cox, D. (1992). Participation and withdrawal among fourth-grade pupils. *American Educational Research Journal, 29*(1), 141-162.

Fowler, W. J., Jr., & Walberg, H. J. (1991). School, size, characteristics, and outcomes. *Educational Evaluation and Policy Analysis, 13*(2), 189-202.

Gardner, J. W. (1995). Wholeness incorporating diversity. *The Futurist, 29*(2), 25.

Harris, L. E., & Harris, R. (1980). *Bootstraps: A chronicle of a real community school.* Cable, WI: Harris.

Heath, S. B., & McLaughlin, M. W. (1991). Community organizations as family. *Phi Delta Kappan, 72*(8), 623-627.

High, R. M., Achilles, C. M., & High, K. (1984). *Teacher actual and preferred involvement in selected school activities.* Paper presented at the annual meeting of the American Educational Research Association, San Francisco. (ERIC Document Reproduction Service No. ED 336 856)

Hochberg, M. R., & Lopez, M. E. (1993). A family matter. *The Executive Educator, 15*(12), 28-31.

Hodgkinson, H. I. (1991). Reform vs. reality. *Phi Delta Kappan, 73*(1), 8-16.

Hoover, S. (1992). *Coping with multiple at-risk behaviors among middle school students through school and systemic interventions* [Major applied research project]. Ft. Lauderdale, FL: Nova University.

Hoover, S., & Achilles, C. M. (1995). What does one look like? A school and community service approach. In E. Chance (Ed.), *Creating the quality school* (pp. 238-245). Madison, WI: Magna.

Hughes, L. W., Achilles, C. M., Spence, D., & Leonard, J. (1971). *Interpretive study of research and development relative to educational cooperatives* (OEG-0-70-2487, final report). Washington, DC: U.S. Office of Education, Bureau of Research.

Johnson, V. R. (1994). Parent centers send a clear message: Come be a partner in educating your children. *Equity and Choice, 10*(2), 42-44.

Katz, N. H., & Lawler, J. W. (1993). *Conflict resolution: Building bridges.* Newbury Park, CA: Corwin.

Knapp, M. S. (1995). How shall we study comprehensive, collaborative services for children and families? *Educational Researcher, 23*(4), 5-16.

Lortie, D. (1975). *Schoolteacher: A sociological study.* Chicago: University of Chicago Press.

Mitchell, D. E., & Beach. S. A. (1993, May). School restructuring: The superintendent's view. *Educational Administration Quarterly, 29*(2), 249-274.

National School Boards Association. (1993). *A resource directory: Interagency collaboration to help children achieve.* Alexandria, VA: Author.

Oakes, J., & Quartz, K. H. (Eds). (1995). *Creating new educational communities* (Ninety-fourth Yearbook of the NSSE, Part 1). Chicago: University of Chicago Press.

Payzant, T. W. (1992). New beginnings in San Diego: Developing a strategy for interagency collaboration. *Phi Delta Kappan, 74*(2), 139-146.

Purkey, W. W. (1992). An introduction to invitational theory. *Journal of Invitational Theory and Practice, 1*(1), 5-16.

Seeley, D. S. (1981). *Education through partnership.* Cambridge, MA: Ballinger.

Seeley, D. S., Niemeyer, J. H., & Greenspan, R. (1991). *Principals speak: Parent involvement* (Report #2). New York: College of Staten Island/CUNY, Principals Speak Project.

SICA News. (1994). Early Childhood Development and Academic Assistance Act of 1993 (Act 135). In *Question Marks* (Vol. 3, pp. 2-18). Columbia: University of South Carolina.

Smith, L. C., Lincoln, C. A., & Dodson, D. L. (1991). *Let's do it our way: Working together for educational excellence.* Chapel Hill, NC: MDC.

South Carolina Council on Educational Collaboration (SCCEC). (1994). *Report.* Columbia: Author.

South Carolina Department of Education. (1993). *A kids count report on the status of children in South Carolina.* Columbia: Author.

Sparks, D., & Loucks-Horsley, S. (1989). Five models of staff development for teachers. *Journal of Staff Development, 10*(4), 40-57.

Stallings, J. A. (1995). Ensuring teaching and learning in the 21st century. *Educational Researcher, 24*(6), 4-8.

Toffler, A., & Toffler, H. (1995). Getting set for the coming millennium. *The Futurist, 29*(2), 10-15.

Yankelovich, D. (1991). *Coming to public judgement in a democracy.* Syracuse, NY: Syracuse University Press.

CORWIN
PRESS

The Corwin Press logo—a raven striding across an open book—represents the happy union of courage and learning. We are a professional-level publisher of books and journals for K–12 educators, and we are committed to creating and providing resources that embody these qualities. Corwin's motto is "Success for All Learners."